Flannelgraphs

To Doreen,

with love
and best wishes,

Joan

Joan McGavin

Oversteps Books

First published in 2011 by   Oversteps Books Ltd
6 Halwell House
South Pool
Nr Kingsbridge
Devon
TQ7 2RX
UK

www.overstepsbooks.com

Printed in Great Britain by imprint digital, Devon.

Supported by the National
Lottery through the Arts
Council England

LOTTERY FUNDED

To John, Catriona and Callum

Acknowledgements:

Some of these poems have been published by: Arts Council South, Arts Council South West, Cane Arrow Press, Cinnamon Press, Envoi, P.E.N. New Poetry, Manchester Cathedral Publications, Obsessed with Pipework, Peterloo Poets, Pitshanger Poets, Poems in the Waiting Room, Poetry News, poetry pf, Poetry Scotland, Portland Poetry, Posterpoems, Prairie Schooner, Radio 4's Poetry Please, The Scotsman, The Red Wheelbarrow, The Mandeville Press, Schools' Poetry Association, South, Second Light Publications, Soaring Penguin Ltd, Staple, Southern Daily Echo and South Hill Park Arts Centre.

Contents

Ginkgo

I pass two beautiful trees almost every day.
Casting around, in your absence, for a way to say
how I feel about us,
I think about them. I discover a fact:
their kind, fossils tell us, has remained unchanged
one hundred and eighty million years.

In the absence of tablets, stone or wax writing,
in this time of separation, of smallness of gestures,
casting around for a way,
shedding my inhibitions like leaves,
speaking for myself alone,
let's say: I feel for you what,
loving all its autumns,
the ginkgo feels for life.

The Real Knack

She'd lost an amber brooch once
and for all in a field of autumn leaves;
a sapphire ring
on the warmest day of one summer
when the sky was blue through and through —
while her great gran's jet necklace went
one especially black night.

But finding contact lenses — her own, other people's —
there she had a real knack.
Cobbled streets, sandy beaches, airport concourse,
even a field where the snow took
a whole day to melt
yielded up, in the end,
from a single blade of grass
the small eye-catching gleam.

Reset

My amber brooch is thimblerigged with leaves, lost
rings are twisted into maidenhair.
My sapphires hang invisible in air.
I cannot split my diamonds from the frost.
It's daylight robbery:
clothed by Cartier, how can I
be seen in leaves and ferns, water, sky?

At Twyford Station

The bicycles are parked like lovers
turned intimately towards each other.
Fresh rain has sweated finely onto the carriage window.
A breeze frees the roses from their flat chintz sleep.
The engine, which has been practising clearing its throat,
turns itself off. We are all between chapters, articles,
waiting to turn the page, eager to fall in love
with this widening calm.
Beneath its surface even the rubbish
speared into the station-master's clear plastic sack
lies like emerald seaweed, sea anemones.

The Nature of Love

Love that is constant is like the flowing of rivers.

Mayoto

The slyness of rivers is as background noise,
their tendency to be there and lull me.

Approaching, at first I think it's rain
and that there will be a day of rain.

In a clearing, I think it's the wind
moving somehow in those trees.

If I defer briefly to other sounds —
when a plane fades, a blackbird boasts

in that rowan, a dog in the valley
barks once —
the river reasserts itself.

My career as a musical instrument

was short.
Already the wound is healing
into a lyre-shaped scar:

a reminder of the moment
when birds kept singing
in the ribcages of bushes
and a wind coming up the brae
balalaika'd the trees
and I, for four seconds,
became musical also.

Out of my hurt leg
ribboned a sound
unsubtle, whistling,
but indubitably music
and so loud that others heard it,
gasped, commented.

Until my heart reasserted
its ordinary rhythm
and the loudness of it ceased
I witnessed, fabulously,
how a new planet feels
at the Music of the Spheres'
sensational one-off gala concert.

Deodand

Darkness and dirt-clog are cataracting the windows
of an abandoned van in Jacob's Gutter Lane

where the police find it.
Tapes like bunting are hoisted, as if to hint it's in
the village summer fayre, half a mile to the north —

uncobwebbed, scrubbed hard, with chintz in evidence,
its cosy interior might invite strollers to peep
at boxloads of paperbacks with broken spines,
the cake whose weight is to be guessed.

*Such a godsend — how it appeared just when
we needed it — the old one quite worn out, beyond repair.*

The local constable, who knows a thing or two,
tweaks his shorts and teeshirt, sticks his head and hands
in the dusted-down stocks, in the throw-a-wet-sponge tent.

Dining with the Dead

They've brought their landscapes with them
as we have our jackets. You can see them,
slipped back from their shoulders, sepia-tinted.

They sit in them, poker-faced, as if seized
by the utter strangeness of being human
in front of this pavilion, beside that table.

They hold paddles, banners, handkerchiefs,
a paused-open book, about which they do nothing.
They're beyond mobile phones, antibiotics.

At our eruptions of laughter,
they're sprayed with a fine mist of food.
Their virtue is not to wince.

At a Distance

Bags ballooned by air gave no clue
other than the names of supermarkets
and besides, who could tell the precise one
he'd carried — contents now dotting the field
behind his house, indistinguishable at a distance
from daisies, the broken bread that never
reached the ducks.

His tight-lipped wife was no help at first
but from somewhere reluctantly brought to us
his diary petering out at the word *philamort*,
its definition *the colour of a dead leaf*
hurriedly handwritten. Also the word *candy*
which we took to be a name.

What photographs there were of him
out of focus, grainy, are as if he were
practising, as if, smelling of peppermints
or wood-smoke, he moves now somewhere
in a socket of sand.

New skills

for the globally warmer world
will include flood wading
taught by out of work
circus performers
ex-stilt walkers
acrobats and the like.

Anger management
will be increasingly called for
with levels of overcrowding
making those living
jowl by cheek
more and more likely
to go for the jugular
of their nearest neighbours.
Our tutors are tried and tested.

Tear control —
though not strictly part of our current
Adult Education provision —
is an old skill;
revision, one-day courses
will be offered
by our highly qualified staff
of tsunami victims,
Haitians.

Ice Driving

The eaves of houses
drip clear blood
down long daggers as we pass.
Not being the driver

I spend my time exclaiming.
Babes in the woods, meanwhile,
in their soaked coats
are muffled,

their feet going out
from under them
and each with difficulty
dragging the other —

as if dealing with
an umbrella in a storm,
inflating and collapsing it —
towards the verge.

Living with the Water-table

Have to keep weeding
the sedge that springs up
at the foot of the drive, where water

comes near the surface. Have to ignore —
or watch out for — the damp shape changes
on the face of the concrete, its darkening
port-wine frown. This past winter

in the long cold, ice held on
for weeks, there, uncompromised —
footfall as certain slippage.

Men came once with a camera
on the end of a long flex, to trace
underground. They advised nothing
could be done; it was the water-table.

Sometimes I dream their camera, swim
down the drainage pipe with the meltwater,
dead rats, lost toys

or flip and paddle back up the hill
towards the source, my feet webbing
as I gasp for breath,
every so often chanting

You, hidden water, can no more
change your nature than the sun can
or the moon, or than I can

with my once-a-year swim in the sea
when the urge takes me to go
back to water, no matter what.

Torn-Word

The torn-word dozes at the root of the tongue,
bides its time, is conformable among
chat, and platitudes and love-sounds
that don't know it's different; while round
uncurls the torn-word, syllables long.
In a sibilant sortie its carefully pronged
fangs poise themselves to slake
with gall and wormwood
the wound they first make.

Steady on there

Because the drunk man
in front
called the two schoolgirls
drifting through the park
in front of him
Black bitches
you said *Steady on there*
then *That's not on*
when he kept on cursing.
You'd just noticed
the young policeman behind
who said *Steady on, there;*
I'll deal with this
glancing over his shoulder to see
if his superintendent, or an angel,
or God, was behind him —
like that feeling you get
in the cloakrooms of posh hotels
when you look in mirrors
and become an infinite reproof
of people who might be you
over the taps.

Neighbours:

1
Doctor Who is landing in the next room

I sit, companionably apart,
pondering the layered landscape of my desk.
Presently I'll go upstairs to check
something I'll remember as I climb
to a study as quietly Tardis-like
as any room, given time, becomes.

It's Saturday night. Around the cul-de-sac
where we live and have brought up children
lights come on like pilgrims' candles, one
then one, as if passed from house to house.

Sue will be feeding the cats, Paula taking her pills,
Arthur being patient with Enid, who's over the hills

2
Because she's dead

there's a young man chopping steadily
at the shrubs near the garage
she always left open
so cavalierly.

Under a hedge a plaque hides
the memory of her husband —
a patient man. Their son will collect it
and the Polish immigrant
clipping so fiercely
may read and understand it,
or not, before then.

She, who'd never take on anyone
except dodgy old men
or keen-for-work students
to do her garden,
has managed, by dying,
to get someone else to pay
for this prompt midsummer clean-up.

Her neighbours pass and wonder
if she's secretly smiling
and the thought of that rictus
makes them almost grieve.

3
Soft

He stirs, on the sofa, from his half-snooze,
Sits to attention, reassembles himself.

Through the wall, the soft striking
Of the neighbours' grandfather clock;

On the piano, the cheerful photo
Of his newly dead wife smiles at him

And on the screen, a sudden split
And crumble in a huge ice-floe

Coincides with something breaking in him —
Softly exacting whatever it is

Courage demands in the scales against itself.

4
A Kind of Acrostic Poem
i.m. Lois Beeson

                    This evening contrives
to make me remember you:
perhaps the way birds are talking to each other
in gardens and my neighbour, afflicted and aware
time for her also is walking out the door,
quietly drinks in her front parlour, where cushions
accept the lessening impress of her body,
the television makes no demands, plants grow
unacceptable in their swallowing of the room's air.

Is it any wonder, given your spirit,
the day before you died we talked so calmly?
Fate was delivering more and more letters for the attention
of the householder onto your doormat, and when I kissed
the side of your face near me it confirmed
dying was what you were about, inimitably.

5
On the Anniversary of the Death of George Herbert

I meant to go to Bemerton today
to walk the marches of your hard-won living
but neighbours, a sick child, got in the way.
I cry excuse enough for my not giving
thought to what your loss of 'Court hopes' meant
and how you worked a life in its despite,
full of good use and temperate content.
Music and marriage swelled delight
but poems measure out the journeys sought,
re-forge the resolutions that you hammered.
You met ill-fortune as we sense we ought,
claimed in the everyday what does not clamour —
the life quotidian, creative and not quaint,
that makes unmythed, unmartyred, the simple saint.

All Lathered Up
for Helen and Patrick McCarthy

Underarming their boards like large, sun-bleached leaves
they'll ask a passing wave to sweep ashore,
young men then paddle to the point where the water changes
colour, darkens to a blue more
dangerous than in the shallows.
They turn and mount.

They've become experts in wave power and water
colours, as you two on your verandah
are experts in the nature of mist on this Pacific
coast. You can tell how it divides
the day, is dried off by the lick
of sun at noon.

You've become people who can take the long view.
Surviving the big fire, you're now to us
the legend of how one refused to leave, the other drove
off down the hill with documents
stashed safely in the car then drew
to a halt. Thought

how she couldn't let the flames sweep him away
— no matter how intransigent he'd proved.
She turned towards the fire line. The car radio announced
relentless news, and all of it
bad. She was there when the fire hit
their garden, stopped

short, burnt itself out at their study window
where we sit, twenty five years on, look down
at the landscape you and the Mexican man from the town
(paid a fair wage, helped in the work)
have re-made between you, slowly.
Strelizia

swallows sunlight as we talk music, books, food
and strategies to keep illness at bay,

while the view lolls to the horizon. Don't despair, you say,
at young folk at the Thanksgiving
dinner who would only discuss
acquisition

and houses, the business of America
being business. Feel pity for them too,
networking in the gym, all lathered up and forgetful
of how, below them, deep below,
fourteen fault lines are shaking hands.
What do they know?

Biography

By the time she had the wit to start counting
One and *two* and *three* and
She was fully awake in the top bunk.
The earth had juddered back into its socket.
So that is how an earthquake feels.

When her waters broke into an Africa-
Shaped stain on the carpet,
Something so wholly physical
Was happening again. On the cusp
Of the pain she craved a sudden

Wholly ethereal existence.
Facing the waves of it laboriously
She held hard to the proffered hand,
Recited childhood poems and watched
A busy urban fox from the ward window.

When she entered a hospital again
To be tested years later
For her fitness to exist
She was halted in the quiet corridor
Of her possible fate — *So this may be it, then* —

And everything around her smoothed down its palms,
Went about its business.
She, it transpired, was standing still
In the slow motion settlement of the ruins,
The gush of a moment after the earthquake

And the pit closed; she walked again
On its surface, lightly, a little gingerly,
Found herself doubly in love with
The sound of the sea in the distance,
The sight of whatever crashed or blossomed at her feet.

Ambition

When other boys think footballer, astronaut,
popstar, he plans for life as a greengrocer,

imagines the round rightness of oranges
in his fist, envisages aubergines

as ornamental as they're edible, and enjoys
the prospect of polishing pearmains

in off moments, also in due course eating
his way through the alphabet — from apricots

to melon to zucchini. He wants
woollen gloves with no fingers,

a green overall with pockets
for his notebook, the pencil

whose rubber band crown shows
it's his, no one else's. He longs

to brush dirt back off the brows of potatoes,
to carry home kumquats in brown paper bags.

The Tremulous Hand Speaks

Sometimes I put a coin on the back of my hand
to see if this once it won't fall,
roll off my desk into the room's far corner.
When I was young I could have balanced

a cup of water there without a quiver.
Later, already started in this trade,
I got ill, but learned to cope.
What else was there I could do?

This was my life — and not as though
I could learn another, by that time.
And they've been kind to me
in their way: they kept me on

and you could say I had a gift
for the work, could see which words
I needed to explain or where to put
the punctuation that would help

some reader in the years to come
make sense
of what those old men wrote.

So no one minds the little jig
my letters sometimes trace across the page,
the way my glosses slope,
and go on sloping, further left

like trees the wind has caught
and keeps on catching
or a woman more and more stooped
under her bundle of sticks.

And lately my brown letters
loop big and even bigger
as if I'm starting to sign off
from this long and busy life

adorning others' thoughts —
a palsied man whose name
slipped, like a lost coin,
in between the minim strokes.

Scullery

She might fall asleep at the sink
if it were warmer in here and the threat
from being careless with so sharp a knife
not so great. The red blood sacs
of the fish she's gutting
tumble down the water from the running tap.

The duckboard she stands on keeps her an inch
from the concrete floor's creeping cold.

Scullery — such an ugly word, she thinks,
till the call from the men for more drink steals
even her solitude. Turning from the opaqued window
she wipes hands on her apron, deftly removes it,
picks up a tray with a bottle half full.
She is, stepping through the door

into the fug of the living room,
two islands out, and swimming.

Anne Caddell
or The Kind of Tragedy it Was

Nothing on the ugly iron plaque —
product of her husband's nearby mill —
records a useful detail.

If she slipped from the bank
mid-sentence, turning to smile
and her skirts billowed rudely
and waterlogged and dragged her
down enough to fill her gasping lungs
and no-one quick enough to save her
and she not quite believing it not a joke
or if she stood alone some moments,
knowing it had come to this:
one seductive leap
into the welcoming arms of the river
would do it, *would do it!*
and no hand to reach for her
gently or otherwise
is nowhere recorded.

Reduced to a name and dates
she lies landlocked,
restored plainly
to a corner of the churchyard,

the kind of tragedy it was
something we won't discover now.

She needs instead daisy chains, chanting
or candles, lilies, a child
to dance on her grave,
someone to scrawl in red paint
aloud
after a century and a half
the graffito
RIP.

Miss Crowford's Bequest

A rich collection

she began on costume jewellery   to purchase it weekly
during her lunch-breaks   then acquired it on her travels
one piece became thousands   meticulous in cases

of artefacts

she recorded each piece in tiny neat writing
her treasure from Egypt India Russia
the pawnbrokers' shops near her Edinburgh office

so strong her concept of a kind of beauty
her devotion to glimmer glitz and sparkle
she earned her own place in history based

on paste and an eye for colour so keen it saw
her yellow Saga badge beside some amber beads
with an egg-sized clasp-stone

brought together

since her death Miss Crowford's bequest
this changing array of gems

she never wore
draws in

from across the world

the lunchtime browser
for bargains of light

One Use of a Painting

When the pain was so bad
he tired of it,
the feeling of helplessness so strong,
going on so long, he felt it
boil in his ears,
he went into the painting:

across the field that might have been a lake
in the foreground, where the wading would be
tough underfoot,
through the big, bright space between the trees
a little to the left of centre
and on —
all in the finest of rain — the kind to be always
just before sunshine, or after it.
At that time he could not tell
which of those it was.

Gunnar Hamundarson's Stumble

We are given to understand
in small doses – suddenly, like Gunnar.
We all may stumble like him.

Two or three times these moments –
leave a country, leave a man,
join another – no forethought, no plan.

Gunnar happened to stumble from his horse
as he quit his home at Hlitharend,
glimpsed his world in mid-air:
how precious the slope's glint,
cloth-of-gold corn, silvering hay,
lovelier than ever before today.
I am going back home; I will not go away.

The outlaw's mind was ravished.
"On pain of death" dulled over.
He saw beyond confusion
and this is what he learned:

we may not know
when the moment of death will be;
we may choose at least its place:
our own home-field, under our own roof-tree.

Dreaming of Havana

When the Lascar seamen
first setting eyes on it declared
the Chief Engineer's face to be *not kind*
he felt subtly flattered,
went on dreaming of Havana.

****

Sheltering under the Hielander's Umbrella
he thought himself back under the arch
where he'd been all at once alone
with a woman who smiled —
her brown bright eyes
the definition of the word *merry*
he'd carry with him ever after.

A yell from high in a tenement
shouldering its way past flags of washed clothes
became the voice from a balcony
in cajoling Spanish that made him want to
answer, if only he'd been able, or dared.
Every other cigar he smoked was the one
he'd tasted at leisure in a sunlit lounge

and sitting through sermons
with his starched collar scratching
made him revisit a phrase he'd been given,
contando la historia del tabaco en dos tomos:
(the minister's spinning a long yarn today)
telling the two-volume story of tobacco.

****

On ships fat with cargo he'd criss-crossed every ocean
for thirty years, survived a world war, maintained
a well-oiled domestic life in a Glasgow suburb,
never losing his countryman's habit of calling Christ
the Good Man and the Bible *the Good Book*

but the scream of a peacock in a hotel garden
the colour and stink of its plazas and colonnades
the gleam of its mirrors and wooden counters
and the way the sea danced with and skirted

Havana had reached him
when his steamship nosed into harbour
that one time, and never left.

Putative Incident in the Life of Onund Treefoot

A force ten gale out of Barra barracked
the captain, laid about the ship like a berserk,
till the slave who'd penned the note
that Onund left for Æsa
saying simply *Gone viking*,
sicked up the words he'd swallowed,
muttered at his master's buoyant swell,
We've sprung a leak!
Then Onund came into his own.
Of Treefoot this tale is told:

he stooped to the gap where the timbers
gaped like a girl's surprise,
thrust his limb in the lacuna,
felt wood judder against wood
as the ship slewed round and ran
under the lee of the wind to harbour.

He was buried in Treefoot's Mound
and on this, and other accounts, folk said:
he was the most valiant and deft
of all the one-legged men who have been in Iceland*.

**from Grettir's Saga, translated Denton Fox and Hermann*
Pálsson, Toronto, 1974.

Reflection

After years of staring
down his no-use beak at goldfish,
his no-use wings growing greener and greener
with the creep of verdigris
and only certain birds deterred
by his motionless presence,
the heron one day
bestirred himself.
He'd been tethered too long to his own reflection.
Something snapped.

Outing the Dirty Linen

Like kissing on the radio his explanation
was strangely unsatisfactory.
It was only later I fully realised.

We were always so busy:
a circus-like marriage, you could say,
keeping all those plates spinning.
Sometimes I was his glamorous assistant,
the one with the slow-motion, brandyglass wrist flick
to avert disaster;
sometimes he was the trapeze artist
who set the rhythm, knew when to catch me.
Everyone marvelled at how we did it.

Now he's gone I think of our dinner parties —
how they lit up, glowed, and our happy exhaustion
afterwards, falling into bed, giggling.

Now he's gone I try to remember her face
from way back, and can't.
To be 'betrayed' for an anonymity
seems, I've concluded, somewhere
between galling and melodramatic.

As I was packing his old shirts for Oxfam
I was strangely moved
at the sight of them.
I decided that, in the hierarchy of recycling,
they'd go in the Salvation Army textile bin
so I could imagine them next to a rosette
of ripped tights and the bags of vomit
drunken teenagers deposit there
for fun, for a laugh, for someone else to have to deal with.

A Corpse Leaves Instructions for a Working Funeral

First you must mend my ways.
Potholes pockmark their length
where my enemies have been run down.
Comb the hedges and ditches;
flush my victims from under stones.
> Tell them all to be brave,
> tell them to dance on my grave.

Next you must fix your sights
on targets other than human.
Contract the swollen bellies
with rabbits shot for the starving.
Restore the grain I kept trampling.
> Tell it to grow in arrears,
> tell it to lend you its ears.

Lastly, don't rake up the past.
Make it a quiet garden.
Re-wind the videos I took
of good men tipped over balconies.
Re-build their unpieced bodies.
> Tell them to pose and smile,
> tell them it was all worthwhile.

Expectation — après Emily Dickinson

Expectation is defined by
hope of things we can't yet see,
like the back view of an angel
or the kite's geometry.

Lovers who endure its torment —
naked swords bisect their bed —
also live by joys repeated.
Meaning stands upon its head.

Expectation is the lack of
radical impermanence
that makes the swan's reputed singing
always only ever once.

The choice of tussore

Though I suppose some notion of comfort
lay behind the choice of tussore
as the silk our school summer dresses were made from,
ironing them entailed
a great deal of effort — mainly on my mother's part.

In this museum the sheerly beautiful
seamless garment of silk
whispers *tussore mysore shantung Xiandong*
and the names of places we may never visit
move through the air
like butterflies in the folds of clothing
carried along the Great Wall from fort to fort.

Shantung

A name like drawing out a thread
that might undo a garment
hardens into a bell
tolled once into thinning air.

The tip of the tongue touches
a ridge of bone
and hardly registers the sound
Shan dong

just as I can hardly tell
if the quick, light touches of your hand
on my arm are to do with concern
or desire.

Touch me again
so that I can trace
what passes along your neural pathways
on the intricate route,

the to-and-fro of silk roads
to your beating heart.
This time I'll pay attention:
a guard beneath a flaring torch.

The Same Latitude

All my life they told me about Moscow,
hurriers by in more, or less, fur,
stamping their feet impatiently,
their breath a visible presence.

Returning to Edinburgh, that summer, I climbed
to the view from a balcony for sitting
and testing the healing power of ether — the bright upper air.
You, in your soft wool bedjacket, sat there gazing
at the aged hospital's onion architecture, its would-be kremlins.

When the tea came in almost a samovar
I took the children home,
chatteringly tired, on the bus
down the Royal Mile,
sitting on the top deck, level
with top storeys all the way, imagining
troikas and you, high also in the gathering dusk,
not really enjoying your food,
living on tea and chocolates

in a ward of dying women
where some were doing it patiently;
some – good fighters in another way — were doing it
as loudly as they could, and with panache
and some didn't know if they were doing it at all

unlike you, mother among the golden globes,
in the amber light,
on the same latitude as Moscow
but beyond the ordinary, bustling cold below.

How Fakirs Feel

Two injections and much drilling later
My tooth is ready for its crown,
For which a careful impression,
In strange cement, has been taken.
Normally self-effacing bits of my head
Have come under unusual scrutiny
While the dentist and I discussed holidays.

Determined to be jovial, supportive,
You propose lunch together, somewhere quiet,
So that if I dribble
I needn't be embarrassed.
We laugh — or you do and I try to
In spite of my thawing jaw.
I allow myself to be overruled,
Wanting something as normal as your company.

But after the first course ends
I bite down hard and chew on
What I imagine to be a leftover chunk
Of cauliflower, or potato croquette
Lodged inside my right cheek,
Only to find it's my own flesh,
Still deadened.

Now I explore the raw, wet skin tenderly with my tongue
And wonder if this is the nearest our culture can get
To knowing how fakirs feel.

A Year on West Hill

The sign on the gate
tells the living passing through
when they can do that.

Smell of new-cut grass
and the spring's importuning
is what the dead miss.

Would the dead enjoy
their sudden, raucous laughter —
those brimful students?

The cut grass drying
in the late summer sunshine —
dead man's confetti.

The house on the edge
no longer contains someone
who lives here always.

Rain on autumn graves
sounds like radios left on
late, in empty rooms.

Here's a magpie perched
on the war memorial,
its uniform smart.

When the wind hugs you
with quite so cold a caress
you know winter's here.

The geometry
of frost-bound cross, fallen slabs:
all over, all over.

Liberty to Fly
'He hath given you liberty to fly about everywhere.'
St Francis of Assisi, Sermon to the Birds, c.1220.

He'd sat in the dark, sat in a quandary,
his mind a jostle of thoughts
as above his head whirred
the thing that made his toddler wake
and cry out.

He'd gone to the room, gone to the place
the child had stumbled from, yelling,
left the light unlit, sat down,
convinced a spinning-top
had taken to flight, was tracing a path
round the walls, noisily

till it came to him:
a trapped swift,
a winged scream.

Oh, the palaver of getting it free:
windows wrenched open, wider,
shooings and coaxings, in the end
a flashlight from out in the garden;
like a man on an aircraft-
carrier, in a film, guiding
the plane downwards — except

this flying thing went skywards,
to slip out of the cliff
it had tried to nest in,
to find a horizon,
the caress of air,
nestle in the buoyancy of air —

yelling a greeting
headlong
into the world's living-room.

Flood Warning, River Almond

Brown fast high past die cast water
Wave and slap branch fall trap rewrite map water

The river smoothes back tresses
of trees like supine mermaids.
The waterfall so much reshaped
boasts its full curved belly.
Four mallards fly for the estuary
direct, as if summoned.

Log drift earth lift stone shift water
All choppy loud stroppy roar floppy water

The weir pool spews its load over and again
and it's not been eating wisely:
squashed bottles, footballs,
tree stumps, polystyrene chunks
arc and arc, as if this river
has made itself bulimic.

No dip don't trip let rip water
All tossing de-mossing no crossing water

Avoiding the spray, three boys
set up their fishing gear, sure-fingered,
by Fairafar ruin. They say
they'll catch salmon in the backwater.
Nothing in this river stays slow anywhere
long enough to be caught.

Sea bound one sound leaf crowned water
Yellow foam free to roam no way home water

River watchers wonder
aloud on the current's height and speed,
voice their nostalgia for its douce old habits,
swivel round for spray
on their stiff waxed jackets
and make this mental note:

Watch your step and keep your head
above it.

Holding On

One gulp would get the eel down the cormorant's throat,
one tremendous writhe win the eel the right
to swim to the firth, down to deep water.
Twice it escaped, twice the sea raven
dived and plucked it out of its element.

All this at the River Almond's mouth
precisely where a Roman soldier
might have witnessed such a struggle,
put a bet, with a mate, on the outcome.
Distracted from draughty guard duty
in a climate neither of them could get used to,
he might also have noted
how a cormorant, on a rock in summer,
on one of those bright, rare days
possible even this far north,
this far away from home,
will spread and hold its wing feathers
to cling to sunlight
like a kind of crucifixion.

On the Ross of Mull

Like a dog on his hind legs, begging
he stared ahead, as if
to memorise the spot
in the air in front of him
he intended to punch

before he dropped, bounded off
in a huge and graceful arc.

Who could predict

his odd quick leaping
from grass hump to grass hump
past brown, clear pools
would look so effortless:
a sort of silent laughter?

A wild hare on the Ross of Mull,
a flourish —

what I remember
of a September afternoon,
that and the coast of Erraid
near but for now unreachable.

Serendipity

Not three princes, or a far-off, palm-strewn isle,
lapped by the Indian Ocean, with lianas.
I think of three sheep, serendipitously scratching
their fleecy bums, wedged woollily,
at just the right height, against the side
of a purpose-built, all-in-one-piece picnic bench
by a beach car-park in North Mull,
their faces showing what can only be described
as extreme ovine delight.

At Calgary
for John

I start up the hill, inland, against the flow
of the fast stream channelled seawards
in its roadside ditch. I trudge. A thin rain mizzles.

Behind me, children jump off sand dunes,
become anonymous
as the wind grabs names
to toss them north and west
towards Ardnamurchan.

Through the now steady downpour
the westernmost light
on the British mainland
guides me.
Its strong beam flicks *home
wards*, then your name's monosyllable.
And I haul myself up on them.

The Wrens' House
at Rubha nan Oirean, Mull

This has become the wrens' house:
twenty of them converse in it,
hop among its still strong stones,
remains of walls that were hewn to last.
They cross its bracken-filled floor space
to explore new clefts. There's sunshine,
a breeze, the sound of the sea nearby.

Nearby, too, the remains of a pier
where people left for good.
Consider the words of a woman named Mary:

It was necessary to depart.
The hiss of the fire
on the flag of the hearth,
as they were drowning it,
reached my heart...

How tiny a wren's heart must be —
not much bigger than a berry,
and the human heart might shrink
round a great pain. In a world
of small survivors, injustice
large as oceans, rank as exile,
wrens keep house for the scattered dead.

They exist in the gaps that are left,
their voices undiminished —
troglodytes troglodytes troglodytes.

Lady

She seems to care for the place,
has the common touch.
We thank her very much
for light bulbs, matches,
delivered, with flourish, to our waiting hands.
She's the lady, it dawns.

The season peters out. Days shorten.
Men fiddle at jobs for next year,
install improbable, rusting gear
shipped secondhand from the mainland.
She supervises, discreetly, tells us
in an undertone: *Donald has it all in hand.*

We marvel at how she handles her going.
For hours sealed boxes are slithered to her car.
In dark Guernsey and skirt she nods, waves far
down to the pier and the prospect of motorways
south, invigilated by lobsters, surprised dead fish.

Flannelgraph

A biddable child, I once attended
a through-the-week Sunday School
in a devout woman's house.
She had scraped-back hair, was kind
and I wanted to see in her sitting-room

for what she kept there: a flannelgraph.
She used it for Bible stories,
placed gently on its grey background
home-made cotton wool sheep.
We willed them to fall off.

And here, half a century later,
somewhere in Glen Lyon,
a second, perfect, upside down mountain
is lovingly placed
on the loch water's soft grey flannel.

What happened to the words on the journey north

I spent some on the calm greenery of Hampshire,
heard myself being pedantic with a few
as we passed Nine Barrow Down
where de Havilland propelled, in this quiet place,
the twentieth century into action.
Motorways lulled me for a long time.
I began to wax lyrical at the Lakes, and at the border.
How were things in Ecclefechan?

From then on I was all gab
and it was only after I'd left Oban,
sailed to Craignure, driven across
the fat foot of Mull towards Fionnphort,
ferried over to Iona,
cycled as far as the north end,
walked the last hundred yards beyond
the last gate and the unchancy looking bull and the last fence
in time for the sunset
with the coast of Mull to my right
and the sky westwarding from there
like the hugest stretch in creation
over Ulva and Gometra and Staffa
and Fladda and Lunga and the smaller bits of Treshnish beyond
and the Dutchman's Cap
that I became at last
speechless.

Other books published by Oversteps

www.overstepsbooks.com